OUR WORLD

Series Editors
Joan Kang Shin and
JoAnn (Jodi) Crandall

Author
Diane Pinkley

D1608971

NATIONAL GEOGRAPHIC
LEARNING

Australia · Brazil · Mexico · Singapore · United Kingdom · United States

STARTER

Scope and Sequence

	0 p. 6	1 My School p. 10	2 My Toys p. 18	3 My Family p. 26
CONTENT AREA CONNECTION	Social and Academic Language, Math	Social and Academic Language, Math	Social and Academic Language, Math	Social Studies, Math
OBJECTIVES	• greet and say goodbye to one another • listen to and respond to classroom instructions • identify and name things that are *red* and *blue* • count up to two items	• identify and name classroom objects • ask and answer questions to identify classroom objects • identify and name things that are *green* and *yellow* • count up to four items	• identify and name toys • ask and answer questions about toys • identify and name things that are *brown* and *orange* • count up to six items	• identify and name family members • ask and answer questions about family members • identify and name rooms in the house • identify and name things that are *black* and *white* • count up to eight items
VOCABULARY ⊙ SC: 1	Hello. I'm [Eddie.] What's your name? Hi. I'm [Freddy.] Goodbye, Polly! Bye, Mia.	*book, chair, crayon, desk, eraser, paper, pen, pencil*	*ball, balloon, car, doll, kite, robot, teddy bear, truck*	*brother, father, grandma, grandpa, me, mother, sister* *bathroom, bedroom, kitchen, living room*
LANGUAGE IN USE ⊙ SC: 2	Stand up. Sit down. Open your book. Close your book.	What is it? It's a [chair].	Is it a [doll]? Yes, it is. / No, it isn't. Is it a [teddy bear]? Yes, it is.	Who's this? It's my [brother]. Where's [Grandma]? In the [kitchen].
CONCEPTS ⊙ SC: 3	Colors: blue, red Numbers: 1, 2	Colors: green, yellow Numbers: 3, 4	Colors: brown, orange Numbers: 5, 6	Colors: black, white Numbers: 7, 8
THE SOUNDS OF ENGLISH ⊙ SC: 4	/h/ **h**ello /aɪ/ goodb**ye** Chant: Hello, hello	/p/ **p**en /eɪ/ **pa**per /ɛ/ **d**esk Chant: I have some paper	/b/ **b**all /oʊ/ **r**obot /k/ **c**ar Chant: Dolls and robots	/æ/ bl**a**ck /s/ **s**ister /uː/ r**oo**m Chant: I love my grandpa!
READING ⊙ SC: 5		Time for School	Birthday Boy	Eight is Great
WRITING PP. 78-90		Aa Bb Cc	Dd Ee Ff	Gg Hh Ii
REVIEW		**Units 1–4**	pp. 42–43	

⊙ BONUS REVIEW VIDEO: SC: 6

GREETINGS AND INTRODUCTIONS

1 **Look and listen.** TR: 0.1

Hello. I'm Eddie. What's your name?

Hi, I'm Freddy.

Bye, Mia.

Goodbye, Polly!

CLASSROOM LANGUAGE

1 **Look and listen.** Say. TR: 0.2

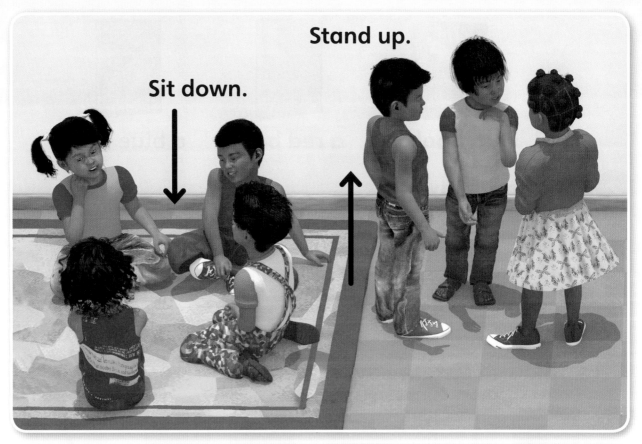

Sit down.

Stand up.

Open your book.

Close your book.

COLORS AND NUMBERS

1 **Look and listen.** Say. TR: 0.3

a book   a red book   a blue book

2 **Point and say.**

3 **Look and listen.** Say. Trace. TR: 0.4

 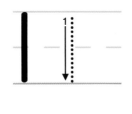   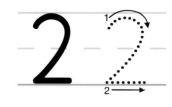

4 **Look and listen.** Stick. TR: 0.5

1	2
3	4

8

THE SOUNDS OF ENGLISH

1 **Listen and say.** TR: 0.6

hello

goodbye

2 **Listen.** Which words have the sound? Check ✔. TR: 0.7

sound	word 1	word 2	word 3
1. **h**ello			
2. goodb**ye**			

3 **Listen and chant.** TR: 0.8

Hello, hello.

Hi there, hi.

Time to go.

Bye, goodbye!

My School

Children make moon cakes in Kaifeng City, China.

VOCABULARY

1 **Listen and point.** TR: 1.1

2 **Point and say.**

a chair

a crayon

a desk

an eraser

paper

a pen

a pencil

a book

Nizwa, Oman

13

LANGUAGE IN USE

1 **Listen and** (**circle.**) **TR: 1.2**

1.

2.

3.

4.

2 **Listen and say.** TR: 1.3

What is it?

It's a chair.

3 **Stick.** Ask and answer.

1	2	3	4
5	6	7	8

COLORS AND NUMBERS

1 **Listen and point.** Say. TR: 1.4

green   yellow

2 **Listen and color.** TR: 1.5

1.   2.   3.

4.   5.   6.

3 **Listen.** Count and say. Trace. TR: 1.6

4 **Listen.** Count and say. TR: 1.7

5 **Listen and say.** Cut out the cards in the back of the book. Listen. Put the cards in the boxes. Say. TR: 1.8

THE SOUNDS OF ENGLISH

1 **Listen and say.** TR: 1.9

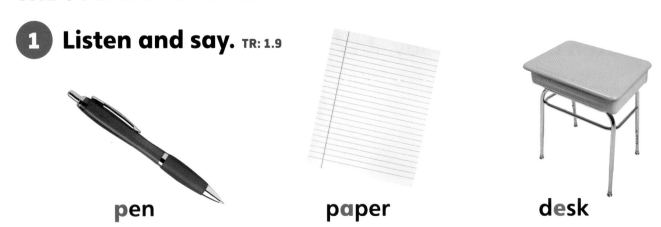

pen   paper   desk

2 **Listen.** Which words have the sound? Check ✔. TR: 1.10

sound	word 1	word 2	word 3
1. **p**en			
2. **pa**per			
3. **d**esk			

3 **Listen and chant.** TR: 1.11

I have some paper.

I have a pen.

I have a pencil.

Let's draw again!

READING

1 **Listen to the story.** TR: 1.12

Time for School

Time for school! Sit.

Four crayons for you.

A green pen for you. Two yellow pencils for you.

OK. Let's draw!

2 **Do you like the story?** Circle.

Unit 2
My Toys

Boy playing with a car,
Dubai, United Arab Emirates

18

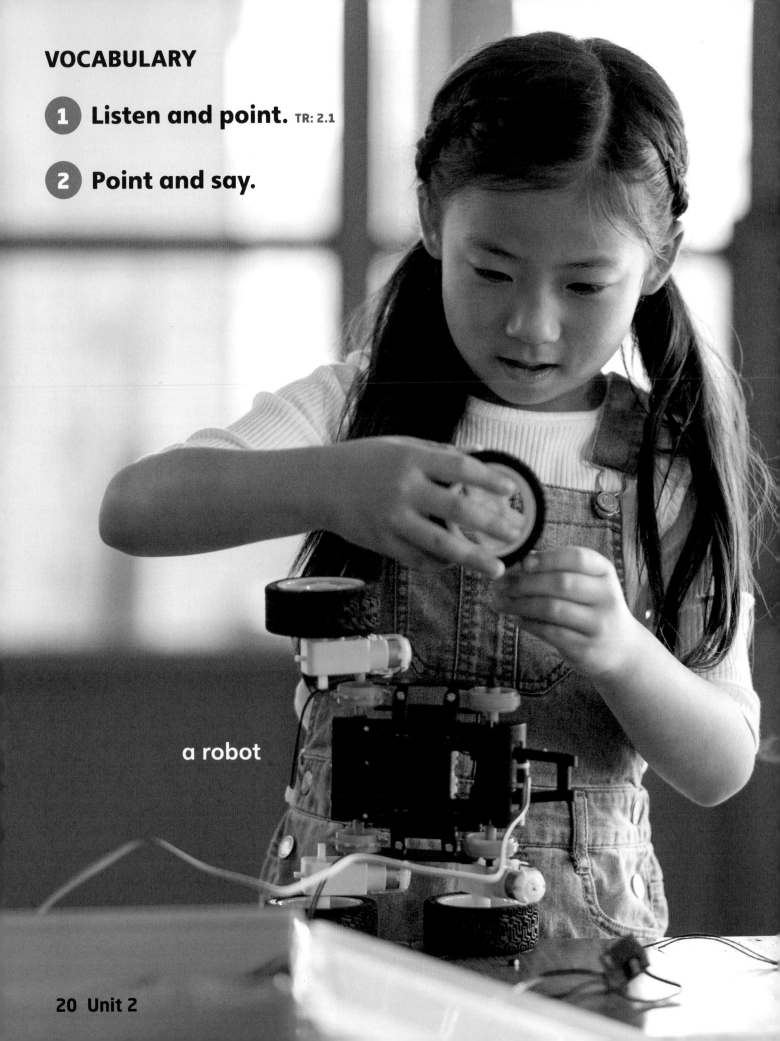

VOCABULARY

1 Listen and point. TR: 2.1

2 Point and say.

a robot

a ball

a balloon

a car

a doll

a kite

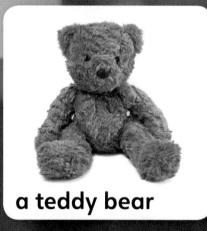
a teddy bear

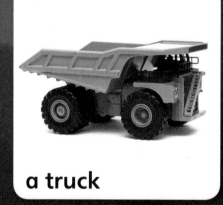
a truck

LANGUAGE IN USE

1 **Listen and** (circle.) TR: 2.2

1.

2.

3.

4.

2 **Listen and say.** TR: 2.3

Is it a doll?

No, it isn't.

Is it a teddy bear?

Yes, it is.

3 **Listen.** Stick. TR: 2.4

1	2	3	4
5	6	7	8

COLORS AND NUMBERS

1 **Listen and point.** Say. TR: 2.5

brown   orange

2 **Listen and color.** TR: 2.6

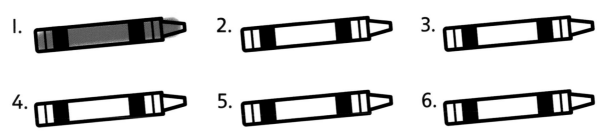

1.   2.   3.

4.   5.   6.

3 **Listen.** Count and say. Trace. TR: 2.7

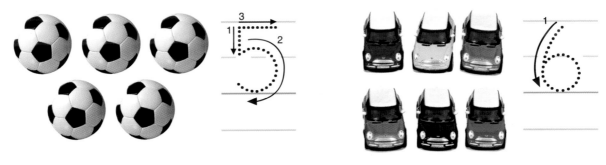

4 **Listen.** Count and say. TR: 2.8

5 **Listen and say.**
Cut out the cards in
the back of the book.
Play the game. TR: 2.9

4 balls.

5 kites. No match.

THE SOUNDS OF ENGLISH

1 **Listen and say.** TR: 2.10

ball   **robot**   **car**

2 **Listen.** Which words have the sound? Check ✔. TR: 2.11

sound	word 1	word 2	word 3
1. **b**all			
2. r**o**bot			
3. **c**ar			

3 **Listen and chant.** TR: 2.12

Dolls and robots
and more toys.
Balls and kites
for girls and boys!

1 **Listen to the story.** TR: 2.13

Birthday Boy

2 **Do you like the story?** Circle.

My Family

Mother and children on a train, Vietnam

VOCABULARY

1 Listen and point. TR: 3.1

2 Point and say.

mother   father

grandma

sister

me

grandpa

brother

a kitchen

a bathroom

a bedroom

a living room

LANGUAGE IN USE

1 **Listen and** (circle.) TR: 3.2

2 **Listen and say.** TR: 3.3

Who's this?

It's my brother.

3 **Listen.** Look at the rooms. Stick and say. TR: 3.4

Where's Grandma?

In the kitchen.

COLORS AND NUMBERS

1 **Listen and point.** Say. TR: 3.5

black   white

2 **Listen and color.** TR: 3.6

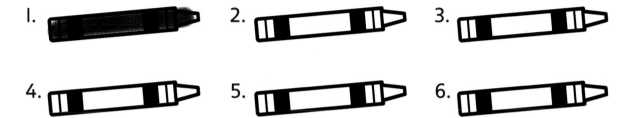

1.   2.   3.

4.   5.   6.

3 **Listen.** Count and say. Trace. TR: 3.7

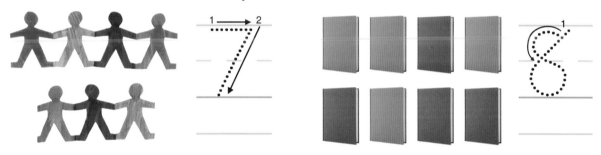

4 **Listen.** Count and say. TR: 3.8

5 **Listen and say.**
Cut out 5 cards in the back of the book.
Ask and answer. TR: 3.9

How many sisters?

Three sisters.

THE SOUNDS OF ENGLISH

1 **Listen and say.** TR: 3.10

black

sister

room

2 **Listen.** Which words have the sound? Check ✔. TR: 3.11

sound	word 1	word 2	word 3
1. black			
2. sister			
3. room			

3 **Listen and chant.** TR: 3.12

I love my grandpa!

Oh yes, I do.

My brothers and

my sisters love him, too.

READING

1 **Listen to the story.** TR: 3.13

Eight is Great

Look! My family is big!

One, two, three, four …

… five, six, seven, eight brothers and sisters!

And eight cats, eight dogs, eight birds, and eight fish!

2 **Do you like the story?** Circle.

33

My Body

The National School
of Ballet in Cuba

VOCABULARY

1 **Listen and point.** TR: 4.1

2 **Point and say.**

Young surfers learn on sand before water.

eyes

ears

36 Unit 4

hair

a nose

a mouth

arms

hands

legs

feet

37

LANGUAGE IN USE

1 **Listen.** Draw lines. TR: 4.2

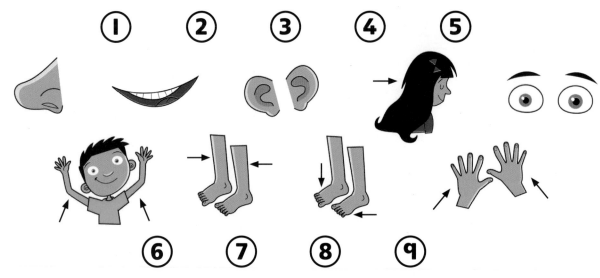

2 **Listen and say.** TR: 4.3

I have two hands.

She has two hands.

3 **Listen.** Stick and say. TR: 4.4

4 **Listen.** Point to the stickers. Say. TR: 4.5

COLORS AND NUMBERS

1 Listen and point. Say. TR: 4.6

pink   purple

2 Listen and color. TR: 4.7

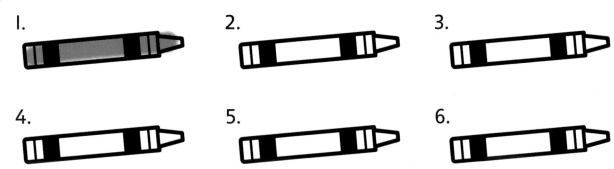

1.   2.   3.

4.   5.   6.

3 Listen. Count and say. Trace. TR: 4.8

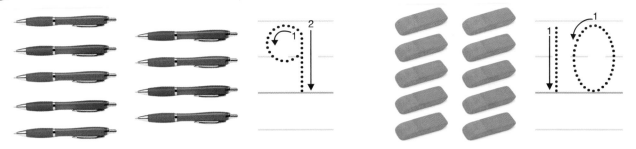

4 Cut out the cards in the back of the book.
Listen. Put the cards in order. Say. TR: 4.9

5 Use the rest of the cards in the back of the book.
Say. Put the cards in order.

2 orange kites.

OK. 3 blue books.

THE SOUNDS OF ENGLISH

1 **Listen and say.** TR: 4.10

arm

leg

mouth

2 **Listen.** Which words have the sound? Check ✓. TR: 4.11

sound	word 1	word 2	word 3
1. **a**rm			
2. l**e**g			
3. m**ou**th			

3 **Listen and chant.** TR: 4.12

One mouth for me,
two arms for you.
Two eyes for me,
two legs for you!

READING

1 **Listen to the story.** TR: 4.13

It's Me!

Mom is in the kitchen.

The robot is in the kitchen, too.

Oh no! A robot with four ears and three eyes!

Don't worry, Mom. It's me!

2 **Do you like the story?** Circle.

Review

Start

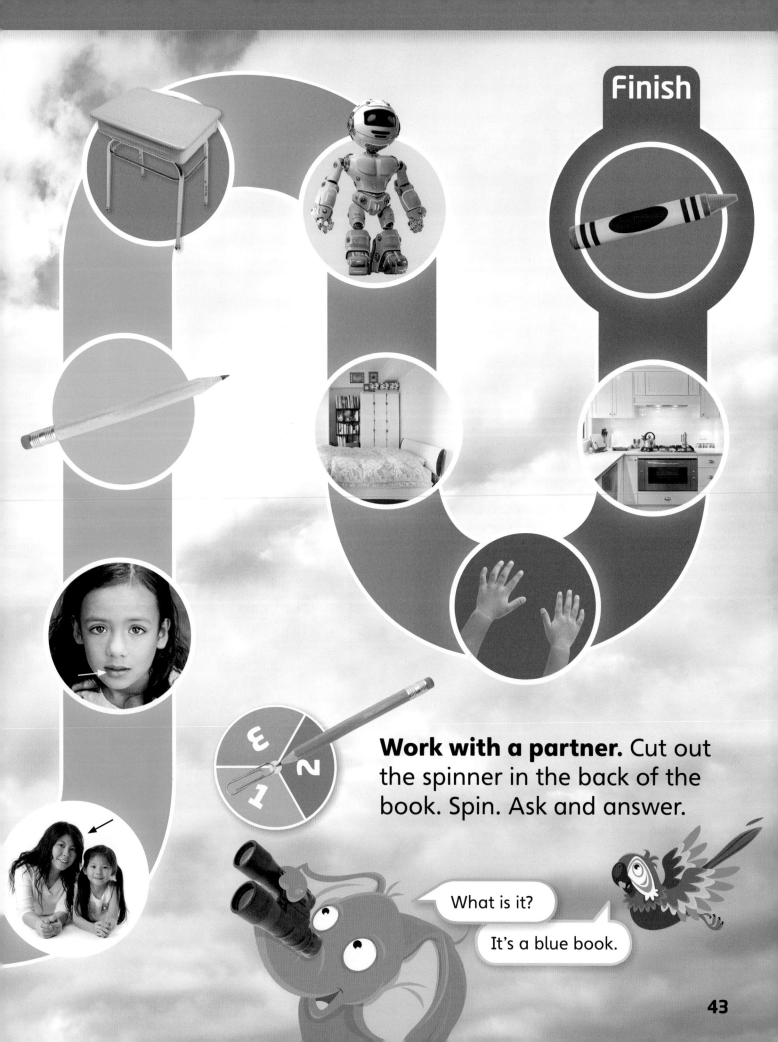

Finish

Work with a partner. Cut out the spinner in the back of the book. Spin. Ask and answer.

What is it?

It's a blue book.

Stories

Neuschwanstein Castle,
Bavaria, Germany

VOCABULARY

1 **Listen and point.** TR: 5.1

2 **Point and say.**

a bird

a prince

a crown

a queen

happy

sad

a princess

friends

a king

LANGUAGE IN USE

1 **Listen and check** ✔. TR: 5.2

		yes	no
I.		○	○
2.		○	○
3.		○	○
4.		○	○

		yes	no
5.		○	○
6.		○	○
7.		○	○
8.		○	○

2 **Listen and say.** TR: 5.3

I want a crown.

I want a friend.

3 **Listen.** Stick and say. TR: 5.4

1   2   3   4

COLORS

1 **Listen and point.** Say. TR: 5.5

gold

silver

2 **Listen and stick.** TR: 5.6

| 1 | 2 | 3 | 4 |

3 **Listen.** Count and say. TR: 5.7

4 **Cut out the game board and the cards in the back of the book.** Listen. Put the cards in two groups. Say. TR: 5.8

THE SOUNDS OF ENGLISH

1 **Listen and say.** TR: 5.9

gold

queen

king

2 **Listen.** Which words have the sound? Check ✔. TR: 5.10

sound	word 1	word 2	word 3
1. gold			
2. queen			
3. king			

3 **Listen and chant.** TR: 5.11

The prince wants silver.

The queen wants gold.

The king wants a crown

of silver and gold!

READING

The Crown

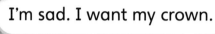

2 **Do you like the story?** Circle.

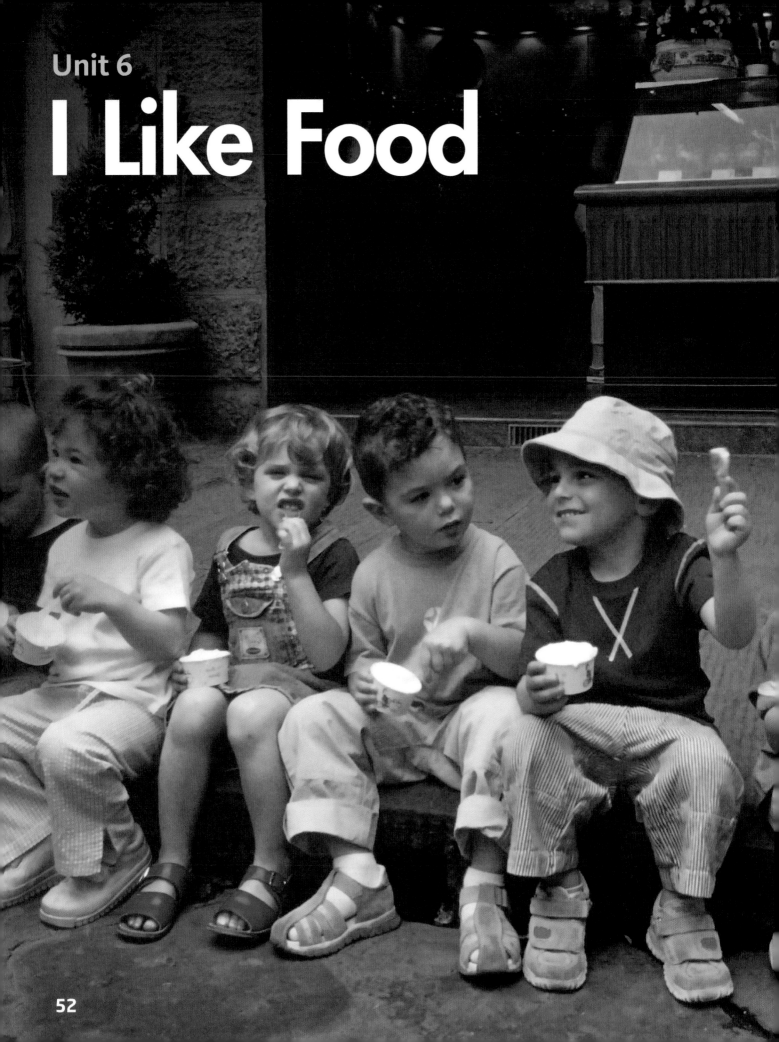

Unit 6

I Like Food

Children eating ice cream
in Florence, Italy

53

1 Listen and point. TR: 6.1

2 Point and say.

bananas

bread

chicken

cookies

milk

noodles

orange juice

rice

water

LANGUAGE IN USE

1 **Listen and** (circle.) TR: 6.2

2 **Listen and say.** Talk. TR: 6.3

I like noodles.

I don't like noodles.

3 **Stick.** Talk.

SHAPES

1 **Listen and point.** Say. TR: 6.4

a circle   a square

2 **Listen and color.** TR: 6.5

1. ○ ☐   4. ○ ☐

2. ○ ☐   5. ○ ☐

3. ○ ☐   6. ○ ☐

3 **Listen.** Count and say. TR: 6.6

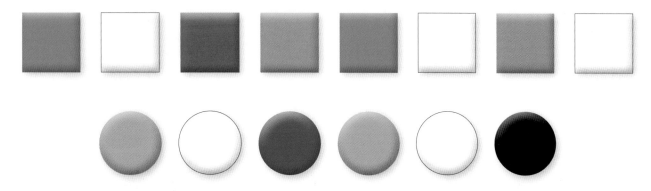

4 **Cut out the cards in the back of the book.**
Listen. Put the cards in order. TR: 6.7

THE SOUNDS OF ENGLISH

1 **Listen and say.** TR: 6.8

chicken   noodles   rice

2 **Listen.** Which words have the sound? Check ✔. TR: 6.9

sound	word 1	word 2	word 3
1. chicken			
2. noodles			
3. rice			

3 **Listen and chant.** TR: 6.10

I like chicken.
I like rice.
I like noodles.
They're so nice!

READING

1 Listen to the story. TR: 6.11

A Picnic

2 Do you like the story? Circle.

Clothes

Los Angeles, USA

VOCABULARY

1 **Listen and point.** TR: 7.1

2 **Point and say.**

a hat

a coat

a dress

pants

a shirt

shoes

shorts

a skirt

socks

LANGUAGE IN USE

1 **Listen.** Draw lines. TR: 7.2

2 **Listen and say.** TR: 7.3

It's hot. He's wearing shorts.

It's cold. I'm wearing a coat.

3 **Listen.** Stick and say. TR: 7.4

1	2	3	4
5	6	7	8

SHAPES

1 **Listen and point.** Say. TR: 7.5

a rectangle   a triangle

2 **Listen and color.** TR: 7.6

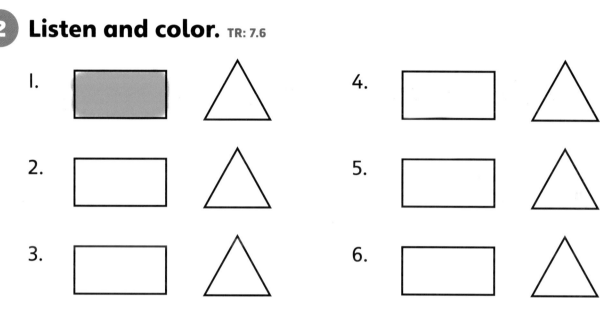

1.

2.

3.

4.

5.

6.

3 **Listen.** Count and say. TR: 7.7

4 **Cut out the cards in the back of the book.** Listen.
Put the cards in order. Say. TR: 7.8

THE SOUNDS OF ENGLISH

1 **Listen and say.** TR: 7.9

shirt

doll

milk

2 **Listen.** Which words have the sound? Check ✔. TR: 7.10

sound	word 1	word 2	word 3
1. shirt			
2. doll			
3. milk			

3 **Listen and chant.** TR: 7.11

I want a shirt.

My sister wants a dress.

Let's shop for clothes.

Grandma, please say yes!

READING

1 **Listen to the story.** TR: 7.12

Wash Day

2 **Do you like the story?** Circle.

Animals

African lion mother with cub,
Serengeti National Park, Tanzania

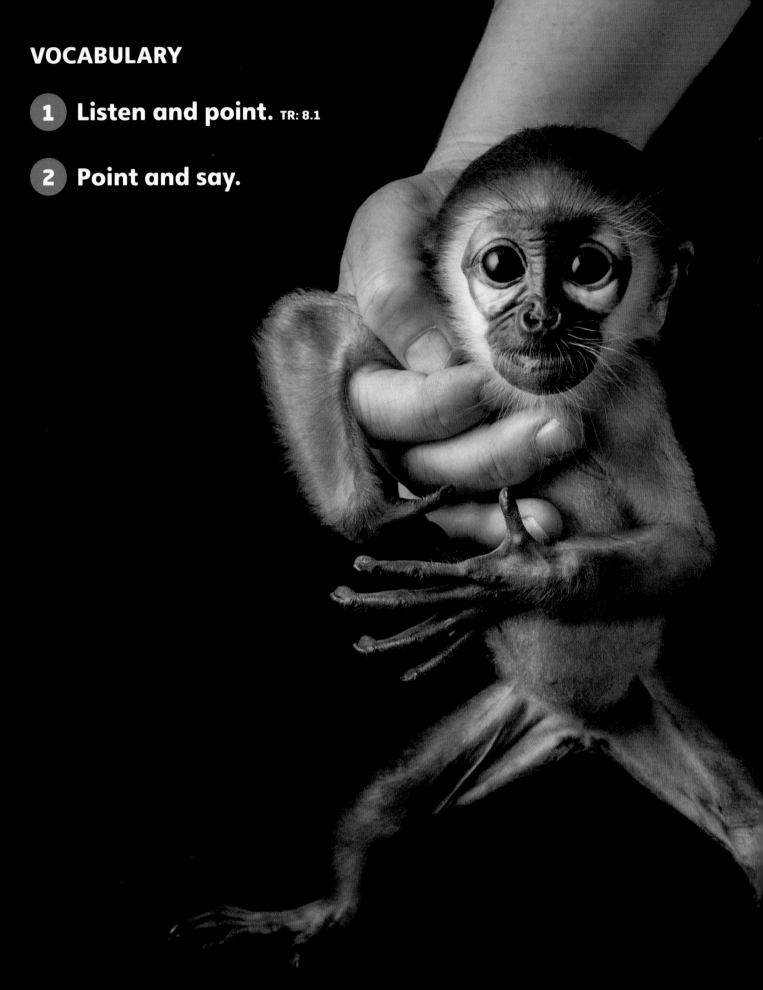

VOCABULARY

1 **Listen and point.** TR: 8.1

2 **Point and say.**

a crocodile

a giraffe

drink

a hippo

a lion

eat

a zebra

run

walk

a monkey

LANGUAGE IN USE

1 Listen and check ✔. TR: 8.2

	yes	no
1.	○	○
2. 	○	○
3. 	○	○
4. 	○	○

	yes	no
5. 	○	○
6.	○	○
7. 	○	○
8. 	○	○

2 Listen and say. TR: 8.3

Is the lion eating?

No, it isn't. It's drinking.

3 Listen. Stick and say. TR: 8.4

1	2	3	4
5	6	7	8

SHAPES

1 **Listen and point.** Say. TR: 8.5

a heart

a star

2 **Listen and color.** TR: 8.6

I.

4.

2.

5.

3.

6.

3 **Listen.** Count and say. TR: 8.7

4 **Cut out the cards in the back of the book.** Listen. Put the cards in order. Say. TR: 8.8

THE SOUNDS OF ENGLISH

1 **Listen and say.** TR: 8.9

run

zebra

lion

2 **Listen.** Which words have the sound? Check ✓. TR: 8.10

sound	word 1	word 2	word 3
1. run			
2. zebra			
3. lion			

3 **Listen and say.** TR: 8.11

Look, I'm a lion.

I walk and I run.

Look, I'm a zebra

standing in the sun.

READING

1 **Listen to the story.** TR: 8.12

At the Animal Park

Look, Teddy. The giraffe is walking.

Look, Teddy. The lion is running.

Look, Teddy. The hippo is drinking.

Look, Teddy. The monkey is sitting on the car!

2 **Do you like the story?** Circle.

Review

Start

Finish

Work with a partner.
Cut out the spinner in the back of the book. Spin. Say.

I want a gold crown.

I like bread.

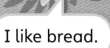

a b c d e f g h i j k l m n o p q r s t u v w x y z

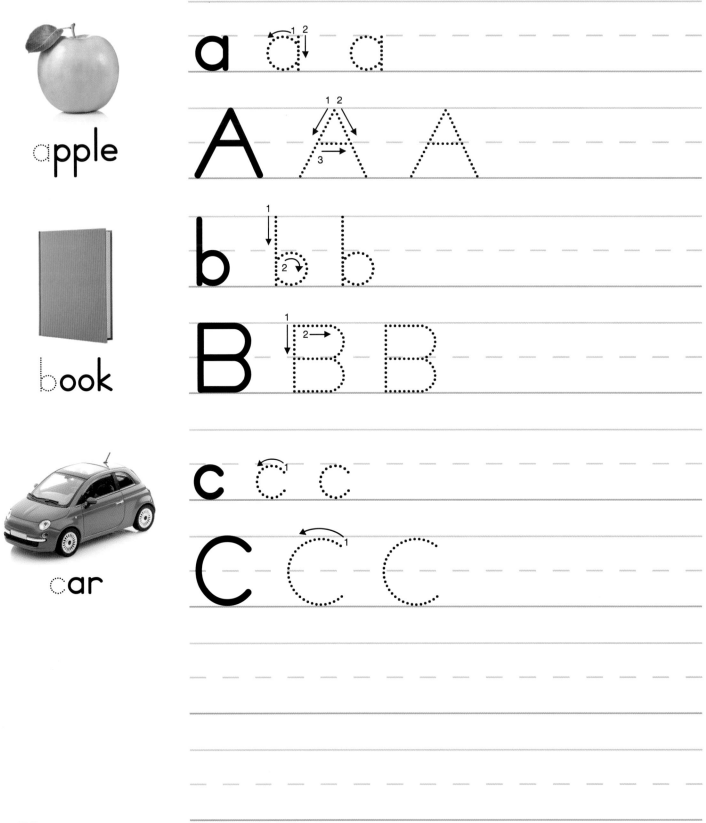

apple

book

car

a b c **d e** f g h i j k l m n o p q r s t u v w x y z

d d d d

D D D D

doll

e e e e

E E E E

teddy
bear

f f f f

F F F F

father

a b c d e f **g h i** j k l m n o p q r s t u v w x y z

grandma

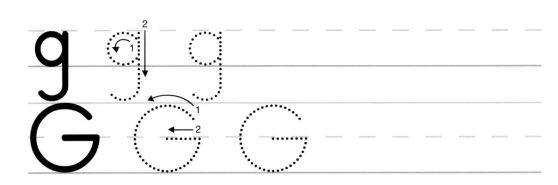

hair

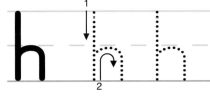

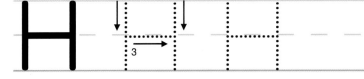

kitchen

a b c d e f g h i **j k l** m n o p q r s t u v w x y z

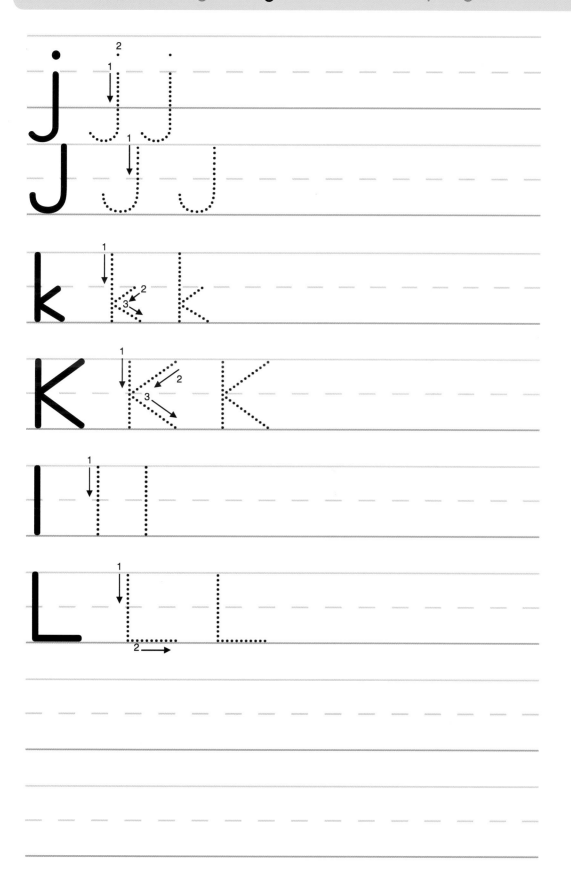

juice

kite

leg

a b c d e f g h i j k l **m n o** p q r s t u v w x y z

mother

nose

orange

a b c d e f g h i j k l m n o **p q r** s t u v w x y z

p p p p

P P P P

q q q q

Q Q Q Q

r r r r

R R R R

prince

queen

robot

a b c d e f g h i j k l m n o p q r **s** t u v w x y z

socks

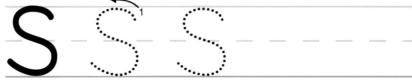

triangle

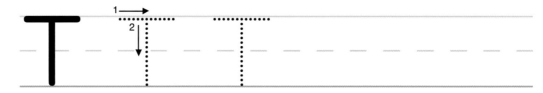

run

vase

a b c d e f g h i j k l m n o p q r s t u v **w x y z**

w w w w

W W W W

x x x x

X X X X

y y y y

Y Y Y Y

z z z z

Z Z Z Z

water

fox

yellow

zebra

Listen and say. Write. TR: ABC9

a b c d e f g h i j k l m n o p q r s t u v w x y z

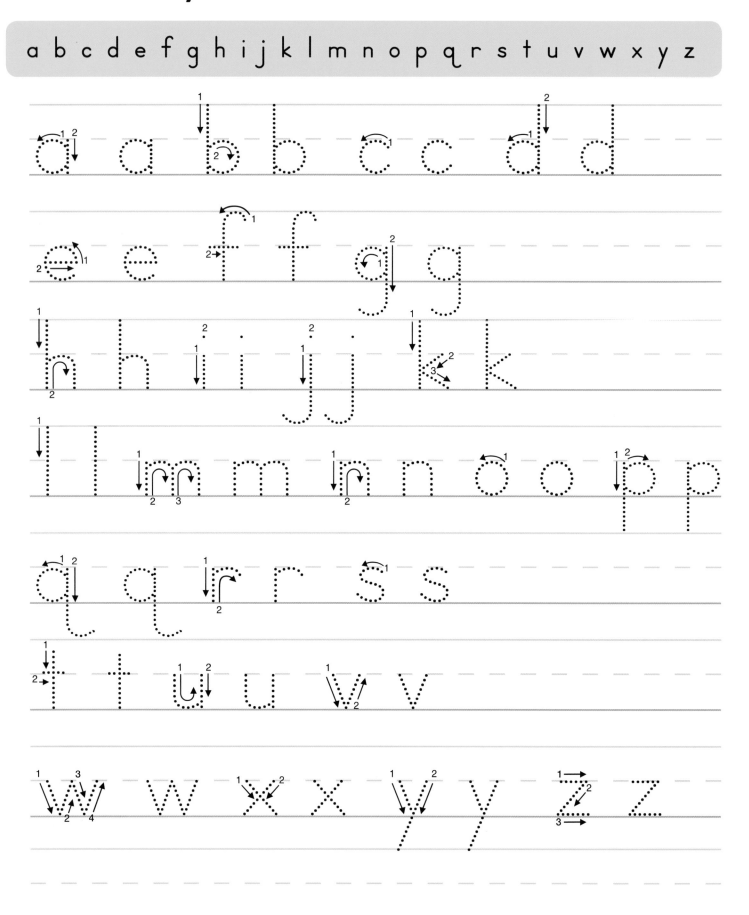

Listen and say. Write. TR: ABC10

Hello!	What's your name?	My name is ...

Hello!

Hello!

What's your name?

What's your name?

My name is

My name is Eddie.

Listen and say. Write. TR: ABC11

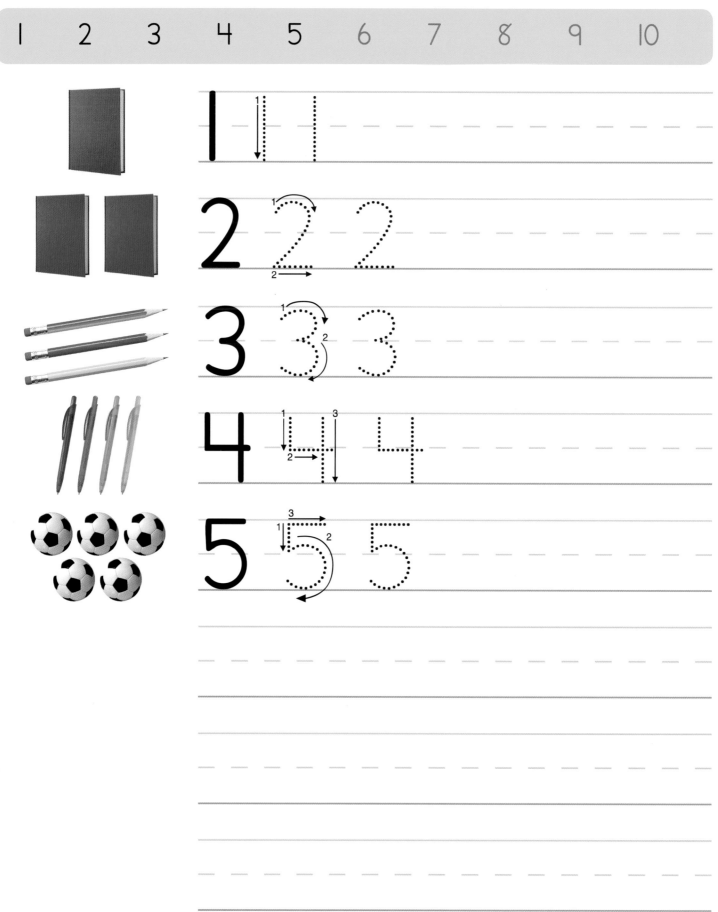

Listen and say. Write. TR: ABC12

| 1 | 2 | 3 | 4 | 5 | 6 | 7 | 8 | 9 | 10 |

6　6　6

7　7　7

8　8　8

9　9　9

10　10　10

green	yellow
blue	red

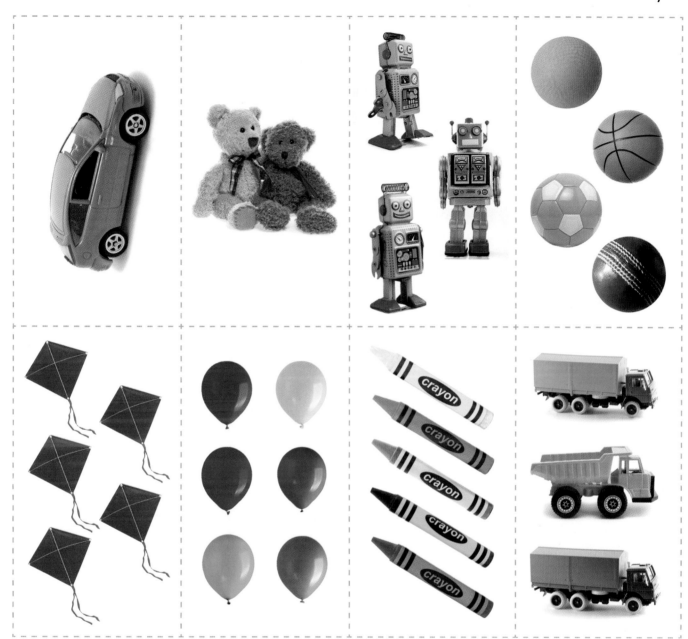

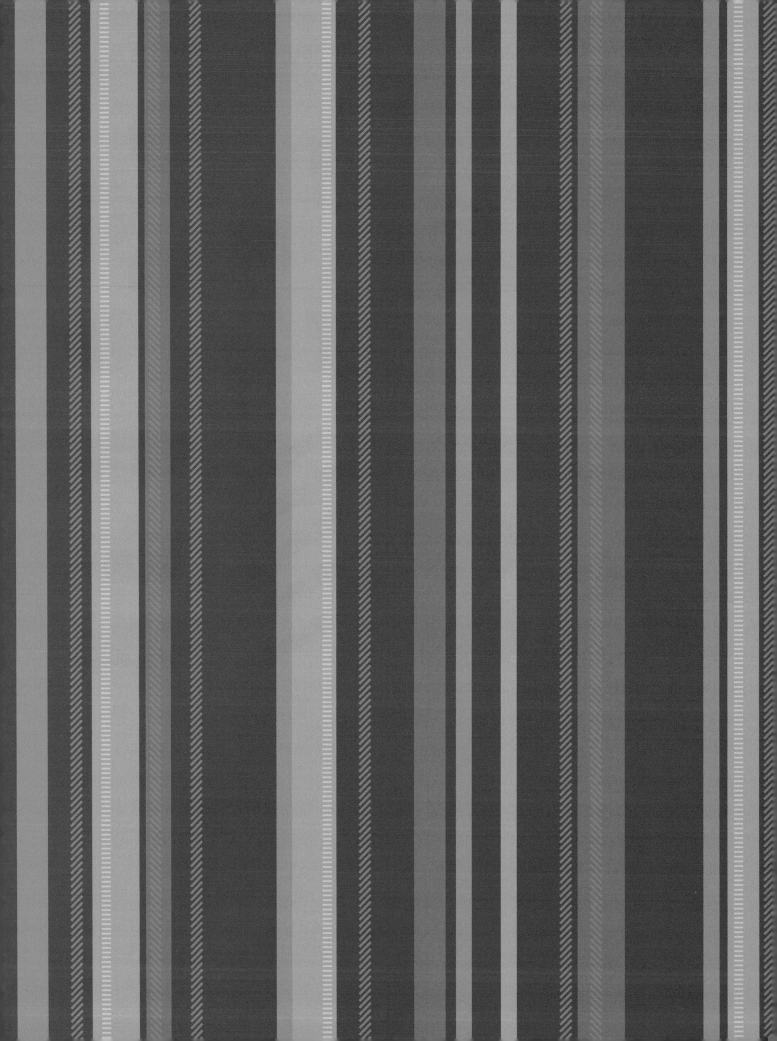

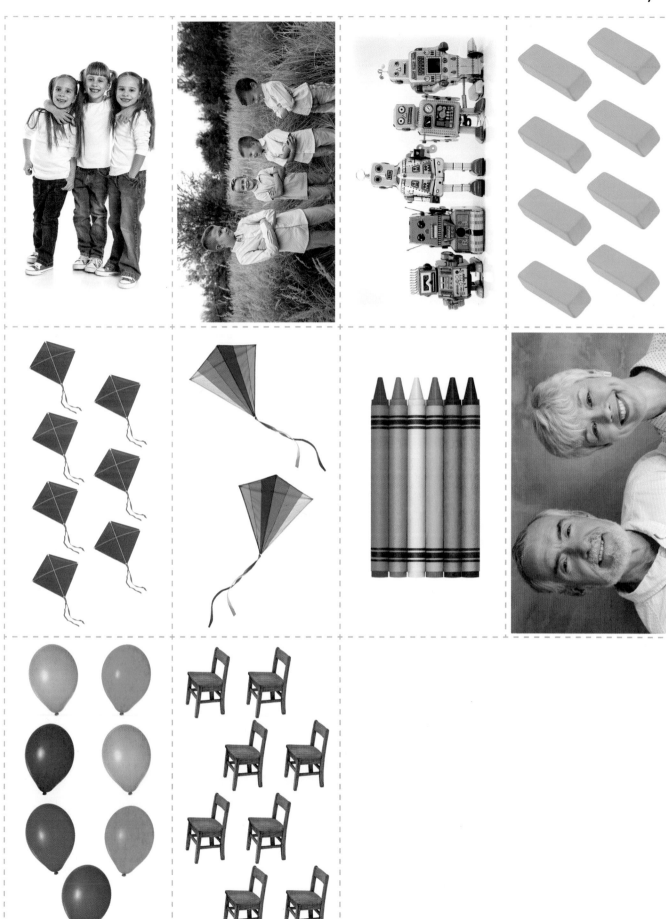

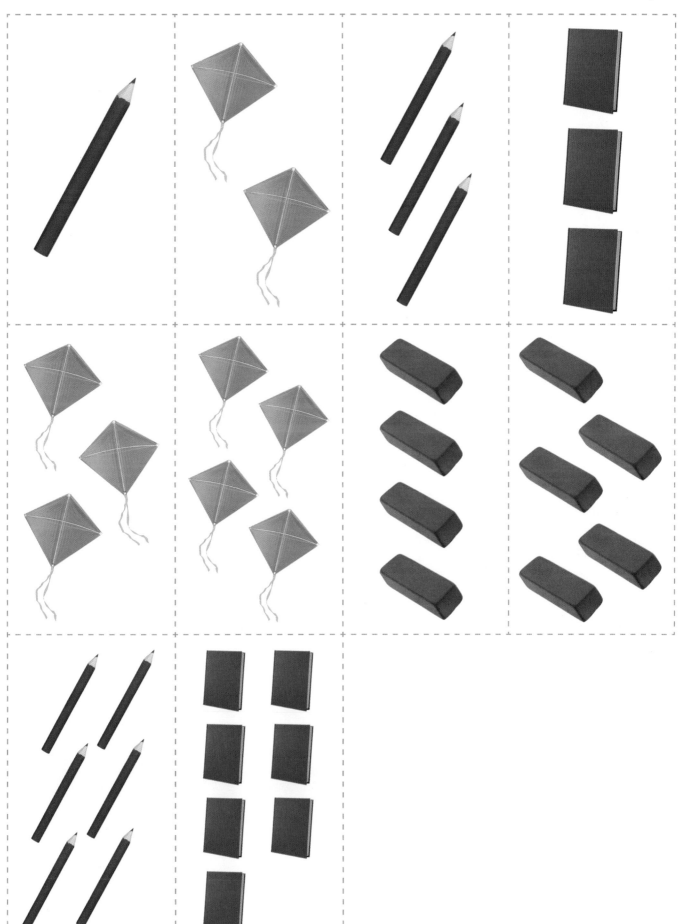

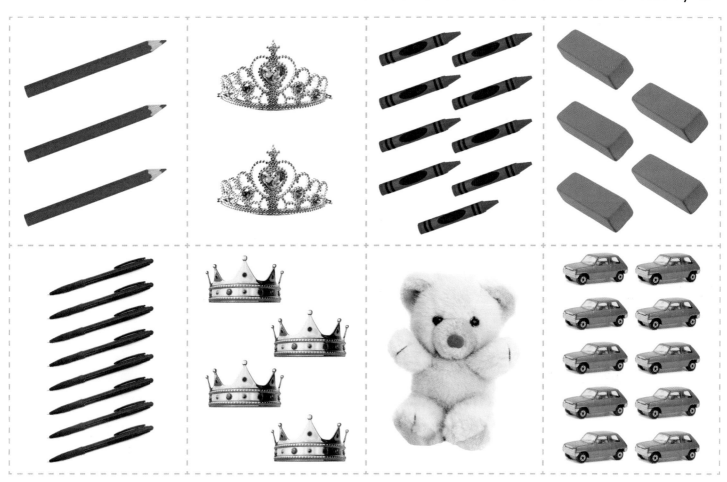

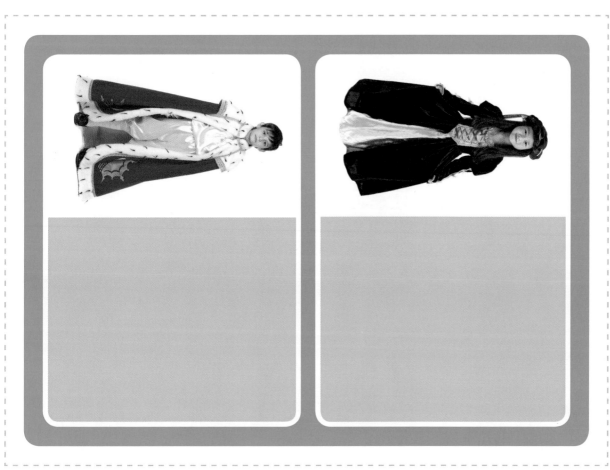

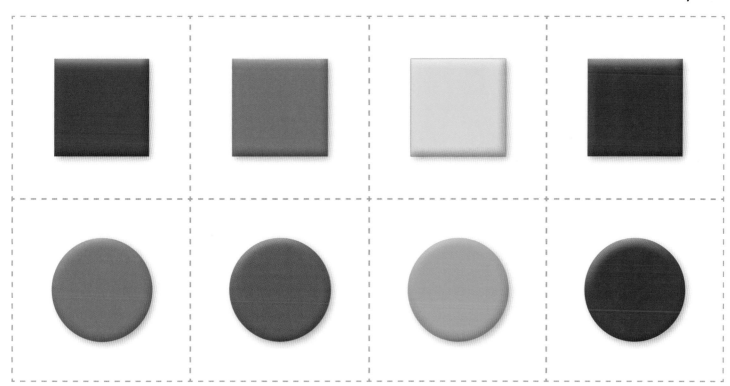

Unit 7 Cutouts Use with **SHAPES** Activity 4.

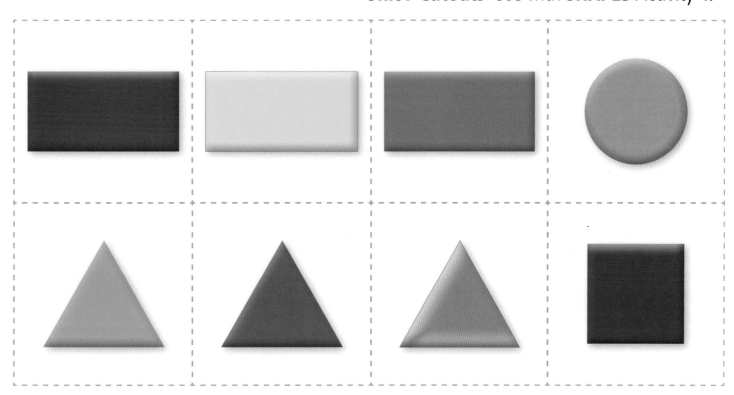

Units 5–8 Review Cutout   **Units 1–4 Review Cutout**

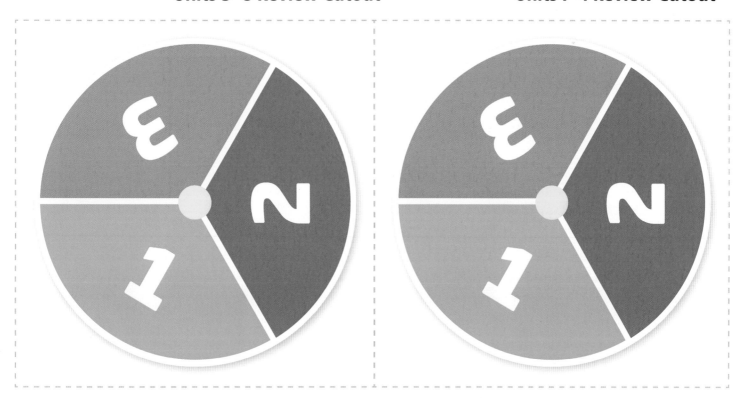

Unit 0 stickers				

Unit 1 stickers				

Unit 2 stickers				

Unit 3
stickers

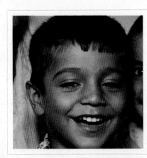  

Unit 4
stickers

 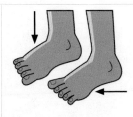 

Unit 5
stickers

Unit 6
stickers

Unit 7
stickers

Unit 8
stickers

Credits

Illustration

Bernard Adnet 59; Scott Angle 32; Tim Beaumont 24, 25, 58; Peter Bull 7; Emilie Chollat 9; Viviana Garofoli 75; Alessia Girasole 50 (tr) (bc), Unit 5 stickers; Amanda Hall 46, 47, 48 (tc), 50 (tl), 51; Anna Hancock 4, 6, 14, 22, 23, 30 (c), 31, 38, 39, 43, 48 (c), 56, 64, 72, 77, 87; David Harrington 33; John Haslam 17, 30 (bc), 38 (tc) (bc), Unit 4 stickers; Corinna Ice 40, 41, 66, 67; Michael Slack 16; Xiao Xin 74.

Photography

4 (ll1) (tl2) © Cengage; (tc1) AP Images/Li junsheng; (tc2) © Mustafa Jindi; (tr) © Catherine Karnow; 5 (tl) © Santiago Barreiro; (tc1) Frank Bienewald/LightRocket/Getty Images; (tc2) Wolfgang Kaehler/LightRocket/Getty Images; (tc3) Peathegee Inc/Tetra images/Getty Images, (tr) Mitsuaki Iwago/Minden Pictures; 6 (tl) (tr) (c) (cr) (bl) (br) © Cengage; 7 (t) (b) © Cengage; 8 (tl) © Cengage; (tc) (c) iStock.com/studiocasper; (cr) (bl) iStock.com/pagadesign; 9 (tl) Michael H/Digital Vision/Getty Images; (tr) B. Blue/Getty Images; (b) © Cengage; 10-11 (spread) AP Images/Li junsheng; 12 (cl) hkeita/Shutterstock.com; (c) Lucie Lang/Dreamstime LLC; (cr) Jeffrey Coolidge/Spirit/Corbis; (bl) Jerryb8/ Dreamstime LLC; (bc) turtix/Shutterstock.com; (br) Kalinin Dmitriy/Dreamstime LLC; 12-13 (spread) © Matt Moyer; 14 (tl1) iStock.com/studiocasper; (tl2) turtix/Shutterstock. com; (tc) Brooke Becker/Dreamstime LLC; (tr) Kalinin Dmitriy/Dreamstime LLC; (cl) Dejan Jekic/Alamy Stock Photo; (c1) Kletr/Shutterstock.com; (c2) spaxiax/Shutterstock.com; (cr) Chris(t)he Testi/Dreamstime LLC; (bc) (br) © Cengage; 15 (tl) (tr) Lucie Lang/Shutterstock.com; (cl1) (cl2) (cl2) Vitaly Zorkin/Shutterstock.com; (c1) © Cengage; (c3) urfin/ Shutterstock.com; (cr) Zoonar GmbH/Alamy Stock Photo; 16 (tl) Kalinin Dmitriy/Dreamstime LLC; (tc) turtix/Shutterstock.com; (tr) Jeffrey Coolidge/Spirit/Corbis; (b) © Cengage; 17 © Cengage; 18-19 (spread) © Mustafa Jindi; 20-21 (spread) JGalione/E+/Getty Images; 21 (tl) Ronald Sumners/Shutterstock.com; (tc) pukach/Shutterstock.com; (tr1) HSNPhotography/Shutterstock.com; (tr2) photka/Shutterstock.com; (c) Andrey Osipets/Shutterstock.com; (bc) Marco Govel/Shutterstock.com; (br) Nikolai Tsvetkov/Shutterstock. com; 22 (tl) Andrey Osipets/Shutterstock.com; (tc1) Ronald Sumners/Shutterstock.com; (tr) pukach/Shutterstock.com; (cl1) HSNPhotography/Shutterstock.com; (cl2) (cr3) © Cengage; (c1) Nikolai Tsvetkov/Shutterstock.com; (c2) Ociacia/Shutterstock.com; (cr1) photka/Shutterstock.com; (cr2) Marco Govel/Shutterstock.com; 23 (tl) (tr) Lucie Lang/ Shutterstock.com; (cl) Ronald Sumners/Shutterstock.com; (c1) (br) © Cengage; (c2) Chones/Shutterstock.com; (c3) Marco Govel/Shutterstock.com; (c4) Nikolai Tsvetkov/ Shutterstock.com; (cr) Ben Molyneux/Alamy Stock Photo; 24 (tl) Ronald Sumners/Shutterstock.com; (tc) Ociacia/Shutterstock.com; (tr) HSNPhotography/Shutterstock.com; (b) © Cengage; 25 © Cengage; 26-27 (spread) © Catherine Karnow; 28-29 (spread) pixelfusion3d/E+/Getty Images; 29 (tr) zstock/Shutterstock.com; (cr1) design.at.krooogle/ Shutterstock.com; (cr2) MIXA/Getty Images; (br) New Africa/Shutterstock.com; 30 (tr) pixelfusion3d/E+/Getty Images; (cl1) (cl2) (cr1) (cr2) (b) © Cengage; 31 (tl) Lucie Lang/ Shutterstock.com; (cl) Dorling Kindersley/Getty Images; (c) (bc) (br) © Cengage; (cr) iStock.com/studiocasper; (b1) Ben Molyneux/Alamy Stock Photo; (b2) Chris(t)he Testi/ Dreamstime LLC; (b3) Dinodia Photos/Alamy Stock Photo; (b4) Nina Anna/Shutterstock.com; (b5) D. Hurst/Alamy Stock Photo; 32 (tl) Wavebreak Media LTD/Corbis; (tc) pixelfusion3d/E+/Getty Images; (tr) MIXA/Getty Images; (b) © Cengage; 33 © Cengage; 34-35 (spread) © Santiago Barreiro; 36-37 (spread) Uriel Sinai/Getty Images News/Getty Images; 36 AFP Contributor/AFP/Getty Images; 38 (t) (cr) (br) © Cengage; (cl) © Anna Hancock; 39 (tl) (tr) Lucie Lang/Shutterstock.com; (cl) Kalinin Dmitriy/Dreamstime LLC; (c) (bc) © Cengage; (cr) spaxiax/Shutterstock.com; 40 (tl) Peathegee Inc/Blend Images/Getty Images; (tc) BLOOM image/Getty Images; (tr) pixelfusion3d/E+/Getty Images; (b) © Cengage; 41 (tl) (tr) (bl) (br) © Cengage; 42 (tl) iStock.com/pagadesign; (tc) Tom Wang/Alamy Stock Photo; (tr) Celia Peterson/arabianEye/Getty Images; (cl) photka/ Shutterstock.com; (c1) Kalinin Dmitriy/Dreamstime LLC; (c2) photolinc/Shutterstock.com; (c3) Marco Govel/Shutterstock.com; (cr1) Lucie Lang/Shutterstock.com; (cr2) hkeita/ Shutterstock.com; (bl) pixelfusion3d/E+/Getty Images; (bc) Asia Images Group/Getty Images; (br) Ronald Sumners/Shutterstock.com; 42-43 (spread) Manuel Breva Colmeiro/ Moment/Getty Images; 43 (tl) Jeffrey Coolidge/Spirit/Corbis; (tc) Ociacia/Shutterstock.com; (tr) Lucie Lang/Shutterstock.com; (cl1) Ron Levine/Getty Images; (cl2) Chris(t)he Testi/Dreamstime LLC; (c1) MIXA/Getty Images; (c2) Happy Together/Shutterstock.com; (c3) Chris(t)he Testi/Dreamstime LLC; (cr) zstock/Shutterstock.com; (bl) szefei wong/ Alamy Stock Photo; (b) (bc) (br) © Cengage; 44-45 (spread) Frank Bienewald/LightRocket/Getty Images; 46-47 (spread) © Amanda Hall; 48 (t) © Amanda Hall; (cl) (c1) (c2) (cr) © Cengage; (c3) James Steidl/Shutterstock.com; 49 (tl) (c) Andreas Fülscher Schliemann/Alamy Stock Photo; (tr) (br) Sergey kamenskykh/Shutterstock.com; 50 (tl) © Amanda Hall; (tc) (tr) © Cengage; (b) © Alessia Girasole; 51 © Cengage; 52-53 (spread) Wolfgang Kaehler/LightRocket/Getty Images; 54-55 (spread) pp1/Shutterstock.com; 55 (tl) Image Source/Getty Images; (tc) Ocean/Corbis; (tr) Alina555/iStock/Getty Images; (cl) (br) Maria Toutoudaki/Getty Images; (c) Seet Ying Lai Photography/Getty Images; (cr) Creative Crop/Getty Images; (bc) showice/Shutterstock.com; 56 (tl) MIXA Co. Ltd./Getty Images; (tc1) Ingram Publishing/Superstock; (tc2) Bo Insogna/iStock/Thinkstock; (tr) HeinzTeh/ Shutterstock.com; (cl1) Lasting Images/Getty Images; (cl2) (cr2) © Cengage; (c) showice/Shutterstock.com; (cr2) Maria Toutoudaki/Getty Images; (cr2) Creative Crop/Getty Images; 58 (tl) Bo Insogna/iStock/Thinkstock; (tc) Martin Lee/Alamy Stock Photo; (tr) showice/Shutterstock.com; (br) © Cengage; 59 © Cengage; 60-61 (spread) Peathegee Inc/ Tetra images/Getty Images; 62-63 (spread) Ramiro Olaciregui/Getty Images; 63 (tl) Dmitri Ma/Shutterstock.com; (tc) Alexander Kalina/Alamy Stock Photo; (tr) Karkas/ Shutterstock.com; (c) dlinca/iStock Unreleased/Getty Images; (cr) John Kasawa/Shutterstock.com; (bc) Magdalena Wielobob/Shutterstock.com; (br) Feng Yu/Shutterstock.com; 64 (tl1) aperturesound/Shutterstock.com; (tl2) Irina Rogova/Shutterstock.com; (tc1) Anna Klepatckaya/Shutterstock.com; (tc2) OZaiachin/Shutterstock.com; (tc3) John Kasawa/ Shutterstock.com; (tc4) Akugasahagy/Shutterstock.com; (tc5) Newlight/Dreamstime LLC; (tr1) kedrov/Shutterstock.com; (tr2) Askjeevs/Dreamstime LLC; (cl) (c) © Cengage; 66 (tl) John Kasawa/Shutterstock.com; (tc) Gladskikh Tatiana/Shutterstock.com; (tr) Maria Toutoudaki/Getty Images; (br) © Cengage; 67 (tl) (tr) (bl) (br) © Cengage; 68-69 (spread) Mitsuaki Iwago/Minden Pictures; 70-71 (spread) Joel Sartore/National Geographic Image Collection; 71 (tl) (tc) (bc) (cl) (c) Joel Sartore/National Geographic Image Collection; (tr) Nick Garbutt/Superstock; (cr) Art Wolfe/Getty Images; (br1) Kent Kobersteen/National Geographic Image Collection; (br2) Michael Greenwood/Getty Images; 72 (tl1) Australian Scenics/Getty Images; (tl2) Gemmy/Shutterstock.com; (tr1) Stu Porter/Alamy Stock Photo; (tr2) Joseph Sohm-Visions of America/Getty Images; (cl1) Ehrman Photographic/Shutterstock.com; (cl2) Alan and Sandy Carey/Getty Images; (cr1) Nicholas Toh/Shutterstock.com; (cr2) Justin Black/Shutterstock.com; (bl) (br) © Cengage; 74 (tl) Rubberball/Nicole Hill/Rubberball Productions/Getty Images; (tc) prapass/Shutterstock.com; (tr) Eric Isselee/Shutterstock.com; (b) © Cengage; 75 (c) © Cengage; 76 (tl) Andreas Fülscher Schliemann/Alamy Stock Photo; (tc1) Image Source/Getty Images; (tc2) Australian Scenics/Getty Images; (cr) Michael Greenwood/ Getty Images; (c1) Sergey Sukhorukov/Shutterstock.com; (c2) © MetaTools; (cl) Africa Studio/Shutterstock.com; (bl) dlinca/iStock Unreleased/Getty Images; (bc1) Nick Garbutt/ Superstock; (bc2) Africa Studio/Shutterstock.com; (br) Mihail Guta/Shutterstock.com; 77 (bl) © Cengage; (c3) mubus7/Shutterstock.com; (c4) onairr/Shutterstock.com; (c5) Chris (t)he Testi/Dreamstime LLC; (c6) © Cengage; (tc2) Creative Crop/Getty Images; (br) © Cengage; (tl) Corbis; (tc1) Karkas/Shutterstock.com; (tr) Digital Vision/Getty Images; (cr) SteveWoods/Shutterstock.com; (c1) Thomas M Perkins/Shutterstock.com; (c2) Martin Lee/Alamy Stock Photo; (cl) John Kasawa/Shutterstock.com; 78 (tl) Lauren Burke/ Getty Images; (cl) iStock.com/studiocasper; (bl) HSNPhotography/Shutterstock.com; 79 (tr) Artmim/Shutterstock.com; (cr) Nina Anna/Shutterstock.com; (br) Tom Wang/Alamy Stock Photo; 80 (tl) 40260.com/Alamy Stock Photo; (cl) stockyimages/Shutterstock.com; (bl) Mixa/Getty Images; 81 (tr) Creative Crop/Getty Images; (cr1) iStock.com/ ElementalImaging; (cr2) photolinc/Shutterstock.com; (br) Bloom image/Getty Images; 82 (tl) szefei wong/Alamy Stock Photo; (cl) Nick Koudis/Photodisc/Getty Images; (bl) Maks Narodenko/Shutterstock.com; 83 (tr) Sergey Sukhorukov/Shutterstock.com; (cr) Image Source/Alamy Stock Photo; (br) Ely Solano/Shutterstock.com; 84 (tl) Africa Studio/ Shutterstock.com; (cl1) SteveWoods/Shutterstock.com; (cl2) Cavan Images/Cavan/Getty Images; (bl) loskutnikov/Shutterstock.com; 85 (tr) Maria Toutoudaki/Getty Images; (cr1) iStock.com/GlobalP; (cr2) Lucie Lang/Shutterstock.com; (br) Lukass/Shutterstock.com; 87 (tr) (cr) (br) © Cengage; 88 (tl1) (tl2) iStock.com/studiocasper; (cl1) Vitaly Zorkin/ Shutterstock.com; (cl2) Zoonar GmbH/Alamy Stock Photo; (bl) Ronald Sumners/Shutterstock.com; 89 (tr) Ben Molyneux/Alamy Stock Photo; (cr1) Dorling Kindersley/Getty Images; (cr2) iStock.com/studiocasper; (br1) Kalinin Dmitriy/Dreamstime LLC; (br2) spaxiax/Shutterstock.com; 91 (tl) Ryan McVay/Photodisc/Getty Images; (bl) Ryan McVay/ Photodisc/Getty Images; (c1) iStock.com/studiocasper; (c2) Vitaly Zorkin/Shutterstock.com; (cl) photosync/Shutterstock.com; (cr1) Lucie Lang/Shutterstock.com; (c2) Kletr/ Shutterstock.com; (cr) © Cengage; 93 (tl) Empiric7/Shutterstock.com; (tc1) iStock.com/ivanastar; (tc2) charles taylor/Shutterstock.com; (tc3) Mikael Damkier/Shutterstock.com; (tc4) charles taylor/Shutterstock.com; (tr1) Mega Pixel/Shutterstock.com; (tr2) Dinodia Photos/Alamy Stock Photo; (tr3) Creative Crop/Getty Images; (tr4) George Diebold/Getty Images; (cl) D. Hurst/Alamy Stock Photo; (c1) Chones/Shutterstock.com; (c2) Lucie Lang/Shutterstock.com; (cr1) Denis Dryashkin/Shutterstock.com; (cr2) photosync/Shutterstock. com; 95 (tl) Max (t)chii/Shutterstock.com; (tc1) khrystyna boiko/Shutterstock.com; (tc2) charles taylor/Shutterstock.com; (tr) Ryan McVay/Photodisc/Getty Images; (c) D. Hurst/ Alamy Stock Photo; (c1) iStock.com/ElementalImaging; (c2) Studio DMM Photography, Designs & Art/Shutterstock.com; (cr) 40260.com/Alamy Stock Photo; (bl) Suslik1983/ Shutterstock.com; (bc) Yuri Kevhiev/Alamy Stock Photo; 97 (tl) urfin/Shutterstock.com; (tc1) urfin/Shutterstock.com; (bl) urfin/Shutterstock.com; (tc2) D. Hurst/Alamy Stock Photo; (cl1) D. Hurst/Alamy Stock Photo; (cl2) D. Hurst/Alamy Stock Photo; (tr) iStock.com/studiocasper; (bc) iStock.com/studiocasper; (c) Ryan McVay/Photodisc/Getty Images; (cr) Ryan McVay/Photodisc/Getty Images; 99 (tl) urfin/Shutterstock.com; (tc1) val lawless/Shutterstock.com; (tc2) Lucie Lang/Shutterstock.com; (tr) Ryan McVay/Photodisc/ Getty Images; (cl) PixMarket/Shutterstock.com; (c1) James Steidl/Shutterstock.com; (c2) Arvind Balaraman/Shutterstock.com; (cr) Soundsnaps/Shutterstock.com; (br) Sergey Sukhorukov/Shutterstock.com; (br) Thomas M Perkins/Shutterstock.com; S1 (tl1) (tc1) iStock.com/studiocasper; (tl2) © Cengage; (tc2) hkeita/Shutterstock.com; (tc3) Lucie Lang/ Dreamstime LLC; (tr) Jeffrey Coolidge/Spirit/Corbis; (cl1) spaxiax/Shutterstock.com; (c1) turtix/Shutterstock.com; (c2) Kalinin Dmitriy/Dreamstime LLC; (cr1) violetkaipa/ Shutterstock.com; (cl2) Ronald Sumners/Shutterstock.com; (c3) pukach/Shutterstock.com; (c4) HSNPhotography/Shutterstock.com; (cr2) Andrey Osipets/Shutterstock.com; (bl) photka/Shutterstock.com; (bc1) Ociacia/Shutterstock.com; (bc2) Marco Govel/Shutterstock.com; (br) Nikolai Tsvetkov/Shutterstock.com; S2 (tl) (tc) (tr) (cl1) (c1) (cr1) pixelfusion3d/E+/Getty Images; (cl2) (c2) (cr2) (cl3) (c3) (cr3) (bl) (bc) (br) © Cengage; S3 (tl) (tc) (tr) (cl1) (c1) (cr1) © Cengage; (cl2) Andreas Fülscher Schliemann/Alamy Stock Photo; (c2) Sergey kamenskykh/Shutterstock.com; (c3) Vladvm/Shutterstock.com; (cr2) windu/Shutterstock.com; (cl3) Drive Images/Alamy Stock Photo; (c4) foodfolio/Alamy Stock Photo; (c5) Iakov Filimonov/Shutterstock.com; (cr3) Subbotina Anna/Shutterstock.com; (bl1) MIXA Co. Ltd./Getty Images; (c6) Ingram Publishing/Superstock; (c7) Bo Insogna/iStock/Thinkstock; (cr4) Alina555/iStock/Getty Images; (bl2) Martin Lee/Alamy Stock Photo; (bc1) showice/Shutterstock.com; (br) Maria Toutoudaki/Getty Images; (br) Creative Crop/Getty Images; S4 (tl1) Image Source/Getty Images; (tc1) Larisa Lofitskaya/Shutterstock.com; (tr1) Zoonar GmbH/Alamy Stock Photo; (tl2) Image Source/Getty Images; (tc2) ESB Professional/Shutterstock.com; (tr2) John Powell/Alamy Stock Photo; (cl) Jupiterimages, Brand X Pictures/Getty Images; (c) rubberball/Getty Images; (bl1) James P. Blair/National Geographic Image Collection; (bc1) Kent Kobersteen/National Geographic Image Collection; (bc2) Nick Garbutt/Superstock; (br1) Jose Luis Pelaez Inc/Getty Images; (bl2) michael nichols/National Geographic Image Collection; (bc3) Joey Celis/Getty Images; (bc4) Roy Toft/National Geographic Image Collection; (br2) Lawrence Migdale/ Science Source; (cr) Eastphoto/Stockbyte/Getty Images.